T0011074

# BASKETBALL'S
## BIGGEST
# RIVALRIES

by Matt Doeden

CAPSTONE PRESS
a capstone imprint

Published by Capstone Press, an imprint of Capstone
1710 Roe Crest Drive, North Mankato, Minnesota 56003
capstonepub.com

Copyright © 2024 by Capstone. All rights reserved. No part of this publication may be reproduced in whole or in part, or stored in a retrieval system, or transmitted in any form or by any means, electronic, mechanical, photocopying, recording, or otherwise, without written permission of the publisher.

SPORTS ILLUSTRATED KIDS is a trademark of ABG-SI LLC. Used with permission.

Library of Congress Cataloging-in-Publication Data
Names: Doeden, Matt, author.
Title: Basketball's biggest rivalries / by Matt Doeden.
Description: North Mankato, Minnesota : Capstone Press, [2024] | Series: Sports Illustrated kids. Great sports rivalries | Includes bibliographical references and index. | Audience: Ages 8 to 11 | Audience: Grades 4-6 | Summary: "From clashes on college courts to big-time matchups in the NBA and WNBA, basketball is an intense game. But what makes a great rivalry? Is it a showdown between two well-matched teams? Is it one player breaking another's record? From slam dunks to national championships, learn about some of basketball's most memorable rivalries."—Provided by publisher.
Identifiers: LCCN 2022048897 (print) | LCCN 2022048898 (ebook) | ISBN 9781669049036 (hardcover) | ISBN 9781669048985 (paperback) | ISBN 9781669048992 (pdf) | ISBN 9781669049012 (kindle edition) | ISBN 9781669049029 (epub)
Subjects: LCSH: Basketball teams—Juvenile literature. | Sports rivalries—Juvenile literature.
Classification: LCC GV885.1 .D6294 2024 (print) | LCC GV885.1 (ebook) | DDC 796.323082—dc23/eng/20221027
LC record available at https://lccn.loc.gov/2022048897
LC ebook record available at https://lccn.loc.gov/2022048898

Editorial Credits
Editor: Alison Deering; Designer: Elyse White; Media Researcher: Rebekah Hubstenberger; Production Specialist: Whitney Schaefer

Image and Design Credits
Associated Press: Charles Rex Arbogast, 13; Getty Images/Bettmann: 5, 6, David Sherman/NBAE, 15, Harry How, 14, Jamie Squire, 28, Lance King, 21, Michael Kovac, 25, Nathaniel S. Butler/NBAE, 12, 26, Ronald Martinez, 18, Sports Illustrated/David E. Klutho, 16, Sports Illustrated/Marvin E. Newman, 22; Shutterstock: 10topvector, 20, Filip Bjorkman, 19, Jansx Customs, design element (lines), Valentin Valkov, 4, vectoric, design element (basketball icon), vectortatu, cover, design element (vs); Sports Illustrated: Bob Rosato, 8, John W. McDonough, cover (top right, top left), 29, Manny Millan, 7, 10, 24, SI Cover/Manny Millan, 11

All internet sites appearing in back matter were available and accurate when this book was sent to press.

Printed and bound in China. PO5379

# TABLE OF CONTENTS

Words in **bold** are in the glossary.

# Rivals Collide

The crowd roars. The clock ticks down. The ball sails through the air. Swish! It's good!

Basketball is an intense game. When big-time rivals face off, the **stakes** are even higher. What makes a rivalry great? Turn the page to find out and learn more about some of basketball's biggest rivalries.

The Detroit Pistons Isaiah Thomas soars through the air during a game against the Chicago Bulls.

# Chapter 1

# Epic Pro Rivalries

It doesn't get better than National Basketball Association (NBA) and Women's National Basketball Association (WNBA) action. The top teams and players meet again and again, creating big-time rivalries.

## Boston Celtics vs. Los Angeles Lakers

The rivalry between the Celtics and the Lakers has spanned more than six decades. It started back in 1959 when the Celtics and the Lakers met in the NBA Finals for the first time. The Celtics swept the series 4–0 to win the NBA title.

Players from the Lakers and the Celtics battled it out during the first game of the NBA playoffs in 1965.

Magic Johnson (far right) put up the game-winning shot for the Lakers during the 1987 NBA Finals.

After the season, the Lakers moved from Minneapolis to Los Angeles. But the rivalry was just beginning.

In the 1980s, Magic Johnson and the Lakers ruled the Western Conference. Larry Bird and the Celtics dominated the East. In the 1984 Finals, Boston squeaked out a 4–3 series win, including two overtime games. A year later, the Lakers got their revenge. They won four games to two. In 1987, the Lakers once again beat Boston four games to two.

It was more than 20 years before fans saw another Finals matchup between these rivals. In 2008, forwards Kevin Garnett and Paul Pierce led Boston to a 4–2 series victory.

Garnett (center) tried to block Kobe Bryant (left) during Game 7 of the NBA Finals in June 2010.

Two years later, the teams met up again. The Lakers trailed by four points entering the fourth quarter of Game 7. But shooting guard Kobe Bryant led the Lakers on a furious comeback. They won, 83–79.

These two powerhouses have gone up against each other in the Finals 12 times. Boston has won nine of those series. Today, they are tied with 17 titles apiece—by far the most in NBA history.

**Stats**

| Regular season games |
| --- |
| 296 (Boston leads 163–133) |

| Postseason games |
| --- |
| 74 (Boston leads 43–31) |

| NBA Championships |
| --- |
| 17 each (tied for most in NBA history) |

| Key players—Celtics |
| --- |
| Bob Cousy, Bill Russell, Larry Bird, Paul Pierce |

| Key players—Lakers |
| --- |
| Jerry West, Magic Johnson, Shaquille O'Neal, Kobe Bryant |

## Chicago Bulls vs. Detroit Pistons

In the late 1980s, the Detroit Pistons were on top of the Eastern Conference. The team was labeled the "Bad Boys." The Pistons often lived up to the nickname with a rough, physical style of play.

But the Chicago Bulls were rising. Led by star forwards Michael Jordan and Scottie Pippen, they were ready to challenge Detroit.

Detroit was too much for Chicago in 1988 and 1989. They knocked the Bulls out of the playoffs both years. In 1990, the Bulls tried again. They pushed Detroit to a thrilling Game 7. But once again, Detroit came out on top.

The Pistons dominated in the 1989 Eastern Conference Finals.

RICK MEARS CONQUERS INDY
SUPER MARIO AND THE PENGUINS
JUNE 3, 1991 • $2.95

Sports Illustrated

FINALLY

MICHAEL JORDAN AND
THE BULLS REACH THEIR
FIRST NBA FINALS

A 1991 *Sports Illustrated* cover celebrated Jordan and the Chicago Bulls making it to the NBA Finals.

Chicago finally got revenge in 1991. Jordan's defense and scoring abilities were unstoppable. The Bulls swept Detroit out of the playoffs. Detroit's **reign** was over. Chicago started a **dynasty**. They won six championships in the 1990s.

## Playoff clashes

1974 Western Conference Semifinals: Bulls, 4–3

1988 Eastern Conference Semifinals: Pistons, 4–1

1989 Eastern Conference Finals: Pistons, 4–2

1990 Eastern Conference Finals: Pistons, 4–3

1991 Eastern Conference Finals: Bulls, 4–0

2007 Eastern Conference Semifinals: Pistons, 4–2

# Indiana Pacers vs. New York Knicks

Sometimes, rivalries are personal. That's how many fans and players felt when the Knicks and Pacers faced off in the 1990s. From 1993 to 2000, the teams met six times in the playoffs. Each team won three series.

Indiana sharpshooter Reggie Miller was at the heart of the rivalry. Miller loved to hit big shots. He also loved to let the Knicks—and their fans—know about it.

Things came to a head in the 1994 Eastern Conference Finals. Miller drilled five 3-pointers in the fourth quarter of Game 5, fueling a huge comeback. As he hit shot after shot, Miller egged on fans.

Miller grabbed a rebound during the 1994 Eastern Conference Finals against the Knicks.

The Pacers won the game, but the Knicks got the last laugh. They went on to win the series with a 94–90 victory in Game 7.

The Knicks Patrick Ewing celebrated after his team defeated the Pacers to advance to the NBA Finals in June 1994.

## Stats

| Regular-season games | |
|---|---|
| 188 (Pacers lead 96–92) | |

| Postseason games | |
|---|---|
| 41 (Pacers lead 22–19) | |

| NBA Championships | |
|---|---|
| Knicks: 2 | Pacers: 0 |

| Reggie Miller, 1994 Eastern Conference Finals, Game 5 | |
|---|---|
| Points | 39 |
| 3-pointers | 6 |
| Assists | 6 |
| Field goals | 14–26 (54 percent) |
| Final score | 93–86 (Pacers) |

# Los Angeles Sparks vs. Minnesota Lynx

The Minnesota Lynx were the top WNBA team of the 2010s. They won titles in 2011, 2013, 2015, and 2017. It seemed like only the Los Angeles Sparks could stand in their way.

The 2016 WNBA Finals was a perfect example. The series was tied at two games each. With 18 seconds left in the final game, the Lynx trailed by one point. Minnesota forward Maya Moore drove to the basket. She drilled a shot to give the Lynx the lead, 76–75.

Sparks players Alana Beard (left) and Nneka Ogwumike (right) trapped Moore during the 2016 WNBA Finals.

Ogwumike (left) drove to the basket during the final game of the 2016 WNBA Finals.

The Sparks charged back. With time running out, they missed a shot. But LA's Nneka Ogwumike reached high. She tipped the ball in, giving LA the championship.

The teams met again in the 2017 Finals. This time, the Lynx won Games 4 and 5. They took the series 3–2.

## WNBA Finals, Game 5 (October 20, 2016)

|  | 1st quarter scoring | 2nd quarter scoring | 3rd quarter scoring | 4th quarter scoring | final score |
|---|---|---|---|---|---|
| Sparks | 17 | 11 | 26 | 23 | 77 |
| Lynx | 18 | 16 | 21 | 21 | 76 |

### Scoring Leaders

| Candace Parker (Sparks): 28 | Maya Moore (Lynx): 23 |
|---|---|

# Chapter 2

# College Clashes

College rivalries can be just as intense as the pros. Students and fans are passionate as the action on the court heats up.

## University of Connecticut vs. University of Tennessee

In 1995, the greatest rivalry in women's college basketball was born. Top-ranked University of Tennessee and number-two University of Connecticut met for the first time.

For years, Tennessee had been the best team in college basketball. But that year, the UConn Huskies stunned the Tennessee Lady Volunteers. They won the championship game 70–64.

Players from UConn and Tennessee tangled on the court during the 1995 NCAA Finals.

It set off an **epic** rivalry. Over the next 15 years, the teams went back and forth. Between 1995 and 2010, they met 22 times. UConn won 13 times. Tennessee won nine. They met in the National Collegiate Athletic Association (NCAA) Tournament Finals four times. UConn won all four games.

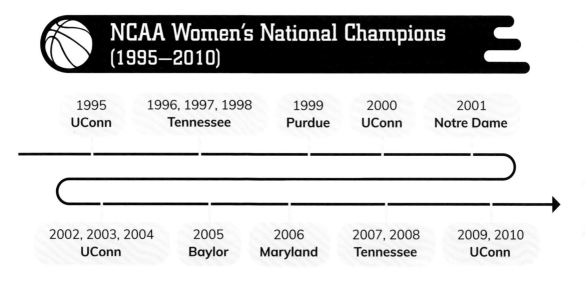

## NCAA Women's National Champions (1995–2010)

| 1995 | 1996, 1997, 1998 | 1999 | 2000 | 2001 |
|------|------------------|------|------|------|
| UConn | Tennessee | Purdue | UConn | Notre Dame |

| 2002, 2003, 2004 | 2005 | 2006 | 2007, 2008 | 2009, 2010 |
|------------------|------|------|------------|------------|
| UConn | Baylor | Maryland | Tennessee | UConn |

### Fun Fact

Coaches Pat Summitt (Tennessee) and Geno Auriemma (UConn) led their programs through their most successful years. Auriemma has won 11 national titles—the most in the history of women's college basketball. Summitt is in second place with eight titles.

# University of Kentucky vs. University of Louisville

These two schools compete for more than wins and championships. They also fight for **recruits** and fans. Located about 80 miles (129 kilometers) apart, Louisville and Kentucky are among the most successful teams in NCAA history.

The rivalry began in 1913. Since then, the teams have met more than 50 times. No game was bigger than their 2012 Final Four meeting. Anthony Davis powered the Kentucky Wildcats to a 69–61 victory over the Louisville Cardinals. Kentucky went on to win the national championship.

Louisville and Kentucky players battled in the 2012 NCAA Division I Men's Basketball Championship.

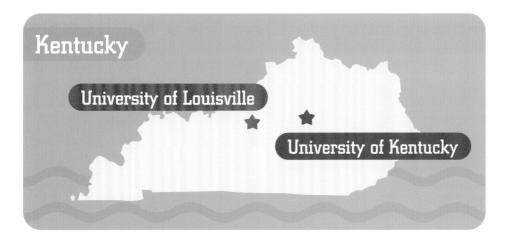

Kentucky

University of Louisville

University of Kentucky

Both teams are among the best in the country. In 2019, Kentucky needed overtime to win the Battle of the Bluegrass, as fans call meetings between the schools. Louisville bounced back in 2020 to earn bragging rights. They won 62–59.

## Stats

| All-time series | |
| --- | --- |
| Kentucky leads 37–17 | |
| **Highest-scoring game (1991)** | |
| Kentucky: 103 | Louisville: 89 |
| **Lowest-scoring game (1915)** | |
| Kentucky: 18 | Louisville: 14 |
| **National championships** | |
| Kentucky: 8 | Louisville: 3 |

# Duke University vs. University of North Carolina

Just 10 miles (16 km) separate Duke University and the University of North Carolina (UNC). But fans are anything but close. Few rivalries are more bitter than the Blue Devils vs. the Tar Heels.

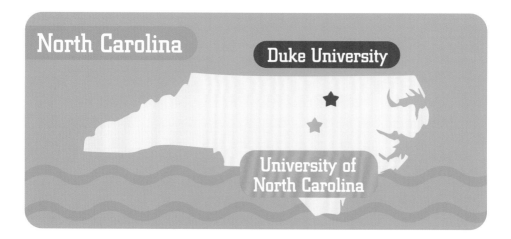

The rivalry began in 1920 and has been going strong ever since. UNC dominated the 1980s with stars such as Michael Jordan. Duke owned the 1990s with Christian Laettner and Grant Hill.

The two programs are among the nation's **elite**. They compete for conference titles and national championships. Their biggest game came in the 2022 Final Four. Duke led at halftime, but UNC charged back. The Tar Heels clung to a one-point lead late in the game. That's when guard Caleb Love drilled a 3-pointer. UNC won 81–77.

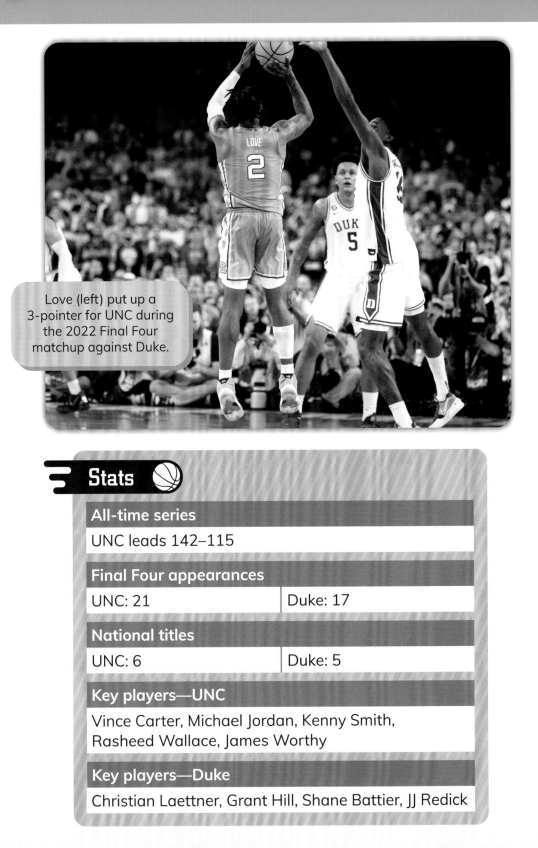

Love (left) put up a 3-pointer for UNC during the 2022 Final Four matchup against Duke.

## Stats

| All-time series | |
| --- | --- |
| UNC leads 142–115 | |
| **Final Four appearances** | |
| UNC: 21 | Duke: 17 |
| **National titles** | |
| UNC: 6 | Duke: 5 |
| **Key players—UNC** | |
| Vince Carter, Michael Jordan, Kenny Smith, Rasheed Wallace, James Worthy | |
| **Key players—Duke** | |
| Christian Laettner, Grant Hill, Shane Battier, JJ Redick | |

# Chapter 3

# One-On-One

Sometimes rivalries are more about players than teams. Fans love to **debate** which player is the GOAT (Greatest of All Time).

## Bill Russell vs. Wilt Chamberlain

Bill Russell and Wilt Chamberlain were the **dominant** players of the 1960s. But aside from playing the same position—center—they were as different as night and day.

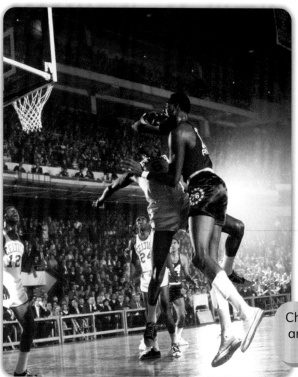

Russell was the perfect team player. He was a defensive wizard with a mind for the game. The Boston Celtics built a dynasty around him. Between 1959 and 1969, they won 10 championships.

Chamberlain (right) threw an elbow against Russell during a 1965 game.

Chamberlain was physically dominant. His skill was unlike anything the NBA had ever seen. He led the league in scoring seven times. From 1961 to 1962, he averaged 50.4 points and 25.7 rebounds per game.

The battles between these rivals were legendary. But who was better? Chamberlain with his unmatched stats? Or Russell with his 11 championships? Fans still can't agree today.

## NBA Career Stats

| Most Valuable Player (MVP) Awards | |
|---|---|
| Chamberlain: 4 | Russell: 5 |

| All-NBA First Team selections | |
|---|---|
| Chamberlain: 7 | Russell: 3 |

| Scoring titles | |
|---|---|
| Chamberlain: 7 | Russell: 0 |

| Career points | |
|---|---|
| Chamberlain: 31,419 | Russell: 14,522 |

| NBA Championships | |
|---|---|
| Chamberlain: 2 | Russell: 11 |

### Fun Fact

Wilt Chamberlain measured 7-feet, 1-inch tall and was nicknamed "Wilt the Stilt." He is the only player to ever score at least 4,000 points in an NBA season.

# Larry Bird vs. Magic Johnson

The 1979 NCAA title game helped shape the future of basketball. Powerful Michigan State faced **underdog** Indiana State for the championship. But for basketball fans, the real matchup was between Michigan State guard Magic Johnson and Indiana State forward Larry Bird.

In the end, Michigan State won 75–64. Johnson and Bird went on to become stars in the NBA. And they took their rivalry with them.

Bird (left) played defense against Johnson during the first game of the 1985 NBA Finals.

Johnson led the Lakers into their "Showtime" **era**. It was filled with flashy plays and big successes. Bird brought the Celtics back to greatness. The pair faced off in epic clashes, including three NBA Finals.

Bird and Johnson have both received NBA Lifetime Achievement Awards.

The two superstars came into the league when its popularity was down. The excitement they brought helped build the NBA into what it is today.

## Career Stats

| Points per game | |
| --- | --- |
| Johnson: 19.5 | Bird: 24.3 |

| Assists per game | |
| --- | --- |
| Johnson: 11.2 | Bird: 6.3 |

| Rebounds per game | |
| --- | --- |
| Johnson: 7.2 | Bird: 10.0 |

| MVP Awards | |
| --- | --- |
| Johnson: 3 | Bird: 3 |

| NBA Championships | |
| --- | --- |
| Johnson: 5 | Bird: 3 |

## Cynthia Cooper vs. Lisa Leslie

When the WNBA started in 1997, the league needed star power. It found it in Cynthia Cooper and Lisa Leslie.

Cooper was a guard who could do it all. She could shoot, pass, and defend with the best. From 1997 to 2000, she led the Houston Comets to the first four WNBA titles.

Leslie was a center. Big, physical, and athletic, she was the first WNBA player to dunk. She led the Los Angeles Sparks to titles in 2001 and 2002.

Cooper (left) and Leslie were honored during the 2006 WNBA All-Star Game.

The two met in the 1999 Western Conference Finals. Leslie scored 23 points and led the Sparks to victory in Game 1. But Cooper and the Comets fought back. They won the next two games and took the series 2–1.

The friendly rivalry between the two helped build interest in the league and pave the way for future generations.

## Career Stats

| Points per game | |
| --- | --- |
| Cooper: 21.0 | Leslie: 17.3 |

| Assists per game | |
| --- | --- |
| Cooper: 4.9 | Leslie: 2.4 |

| Rebounds per game | |
| --- | --- |
| Cooper: 3.3 | Leslie: 9.1 |

| MVP Awards | |
| --- | --- |
| Cooper: 2 | Leslie: 3 |

| WNBA Championships | |
| --- | --- |
| Cooper: 4 | Leslie: 2 |

# Kobe Bryant vs. LeBron James vs. Michael Jordan

Who is the GOAT? For many fans, the debate centers on Michael Jordan, Kobe Bryant, and LeBron James.

Jordan came first, dominating the 1990s. Bryant entered the league in 1996. The two clashed in the 2003 All-Star Game. It was Jordan's final season. He scored 20 points in the game. But Bryant scored 22, leading the Western Conference to victory.

Jordan (left) and Bryant are considered two of the best players of all time.

James entered the league in 2003. He and Bryant squared off many times. Fans loved to debate who was better. Bryant was the better pure scorer. But James' all-around game made him a force in the league.

Bryant (left) and James faced off in a 2009 game between the Los Angeles Lakers and the Cleveland Cavaliers.

Who's the best? Jordan, Bryant, James, or someone else? The rivalry lives on as fans discuss three legendary careers.

## Career Stats

| Scoring titles | | |
|---|---|---|
| Jordan: 10 | Bryant: 2 | James: 1 |
| **MVP Awards** | | |
| Jordan: 5 | Bryant: 1 | James: 4 |
| **NBA All-Star selections** | | |
| Jordan: 14 | Bryant: 18 | James: 18 |
| **NBA Championships** | | |
| Jordan: 6 | Bryant: 5 | James: 4 |

# Glossary

**debate** (di-BATE)—a discussion between two sides with different ways of thinking on a subject; each side tries to convince people that it is right

**dominant** (DOM-uh-nuhnt)—to win in a way that looks or seems easy

**dynasty** (DYE-nuh-stee)—a team that wins multiple championships over a period of several years

**elite** (i-LEET)—describes players who are among the best in the league

**epic** (EP-ik)—heroic or impressive because of great size or effort

**era** (ER-uh)—a period of time starting from a special date or event or known for a certain feature

**recruit** (ri-KROOT)—a high-school player preparing to join a college team

**reign** (REYN)—the time during which someone is the best or most powerful

**stakes** (STEYKS)—the prize in a contest

**underdog** (UHN-der-dawg)—a person or team that is not expected to win an event

# Read More

Berglund, Bruce. *Basketball GOATs: The Greatest Athletes of All Time*. North Mankato, MN: Capstone Press, 2022.

Davidson, B. Keith. *WNBA*. New York: Crabtree Publishing, 2021.

Doeden, Matt. *Basketball Greats*. North Mankato, MN: Capstone Press, 2022.

Scheff, Matt. *NBA and WNBA Finals: Basketball's Biggest Playoffs*. Minneapolis: Lerner Publications, 2021.

# Internet Sites

*NBA History*
nba.com/history

*Sports Illustrated Kids: Basketball*
sikids.com/basketball

*WNBA*
wnba.com

# Index

# About the Author

**Matt Doeden** is a freelance author and editor from Minnesota. He has written numerous children's books on sports, music, current events, the military, extreme survival, and much more. His books *Basketball Shoes, Shorts, and Style; Dragons;* and *Could You Be a Monster Wave Surfer?* (all by Capstone Press) are Junior Library Guild selections. Doeden began his career as a sportswriter before turning to publishing. He lives in Minnesota with his wife and two children.

photo credit: Tracy Caffery